Fantasy Science Field Trips

A Day Inside the Human Body

Claire Throp

Raintree

© 2014 Raintree
an imprint of Capstone Global Library, LLC
Chicago, Illinois

To contact Capstone Global Library, please call 800-747-4992,
or visit our web site www.capstonepub.com

Edited by Dan Nunn and Catherine Veitch
Designed by Cynthia Akiyoshi
Picture research by Ruth Blair
Production by Vicki Fitzgerald
Originated by Capstone Global Library Limited

Library of Congress Cataloging-in-Publication Data
Throp, Claire.
A Day inside the human body / Claire Throp.
     pages cm.—(Fantasy field trips)
  Includes bibliographical references and index.
  ISBN 978-1-4109-6199-0 (hb)—ISBN 978-1-4109-6204-1 (pb)
1. Human body—Juvenile literature 2. Human physiology—Juvenile
literature. 3. Human anatomy—Juvenile literature. I. Title.
  QP37.T575 2014
  612—dc23   2013012669

Image Credits
Almay Stock Photo: MedicalRF.com, 13; Getty Images: leonello,
11, Randy Faris, 5 right; Shutterstock: 2xSamara.com, 29, Andrea
Danti, 21, Andrey Armyagov, 24, AnneMS, 27, Asier Romero, cover,
caesart, design element, chatursunil, 25, grafnata, 7, Makhnach_S,
design element, Palo_ok, 28, Sebastian Kaulitzki, 19, Tyler Olson,
15, wonderisland, 20, Yuri Arcurs, 26; SuperStock: Daghlian/Phanie,
8, Greg Gerla/age fotostock, 6, JACOPIN/BSIP, 14, 23, Radius, 5 left,
Science Photo Library, 4, 9, 10, 16, 17, Science Picture Company, 1,
12, 18, Science Picture Company/Science Faction, 22

Some words are shown in bold, **like this**.
You can find out what they mean by
looking in the glossary.

Contents

Let's Travel Around the Body!

We're going to travel all around the body in just one day! It's time to board our amazing, magical shrinking rocket.

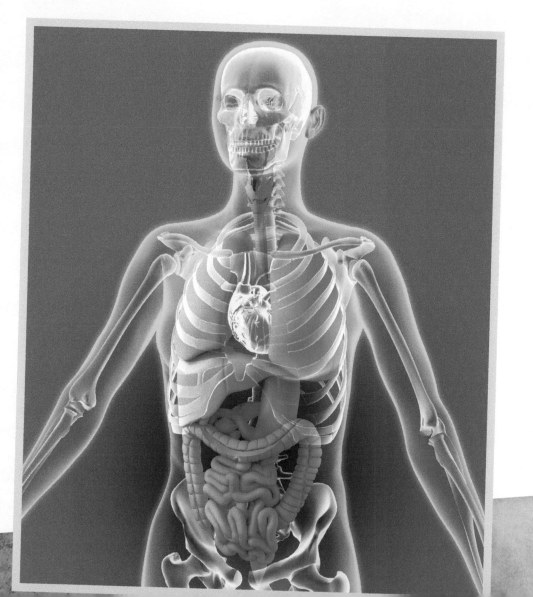

Put on your space suit and jump aboard...

Teeth

Our journey starts in the mouth. Adults have 32 teeth that are used to chew food. The liquid in your mouth is called **saliva**. It mixes with the food and makes the food softer so that it can be swallowed.

taste bud

The tongue is covered
in up to 10,000 taste
buds. These are used
for tasting food.

Lungs

When you breathe in, air moves through the windpipe into the lungs. That is where we are going to steer our rocket next. The air contains a gas called **oxygen**. The lungs pass this oxygen to your blood. You need oxygen to live.

hairs

Steer clear of the tiny hairs in the windpipe! These hairs trap dirt and stop it from reaching the lungs.

Did you know?

Your left lung is slightly smaller than your right because it has to leave room for the heart.

heart

windpipe

lungs

Heart

Our next stop is the heart. The heart is one of the most important **organs** of the body. The heart's job is to pump blood around the body through special tubes called **blood vessels**.

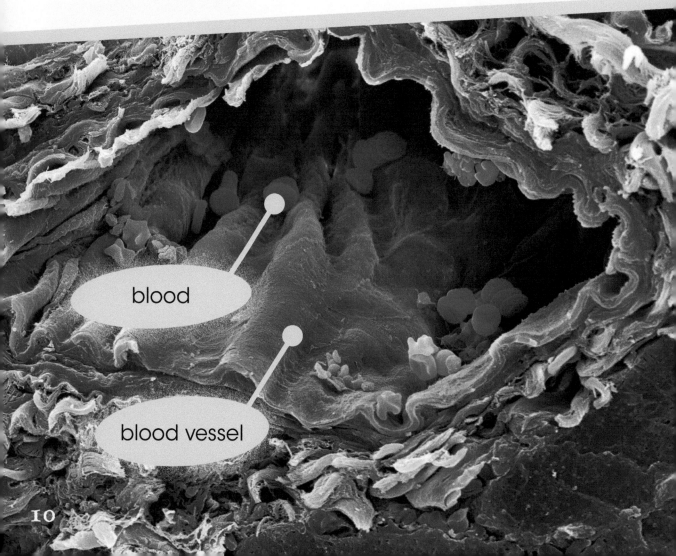

blood

blood vessel

heart

Blood

Hold on tight! Our rocket is going to be swishing along in some blood for a while. Blood is made up of red blood **cells**, white blood cells, and **platelets**.

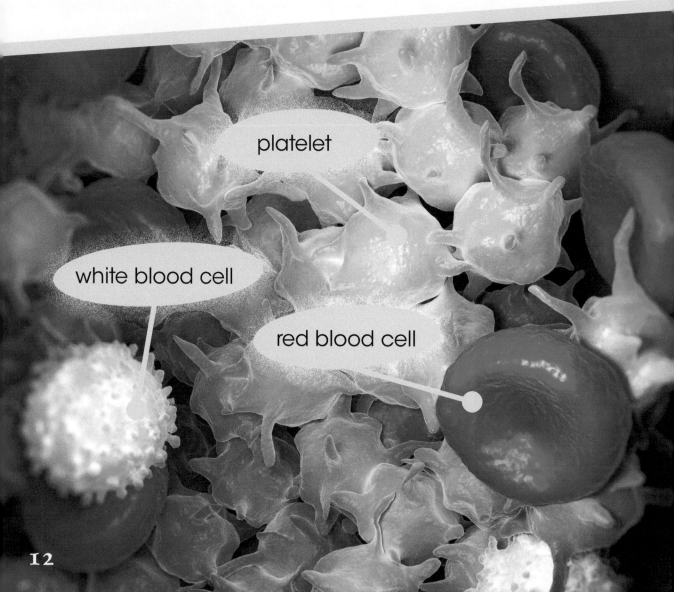

platelet

white blood cell

red blood cell

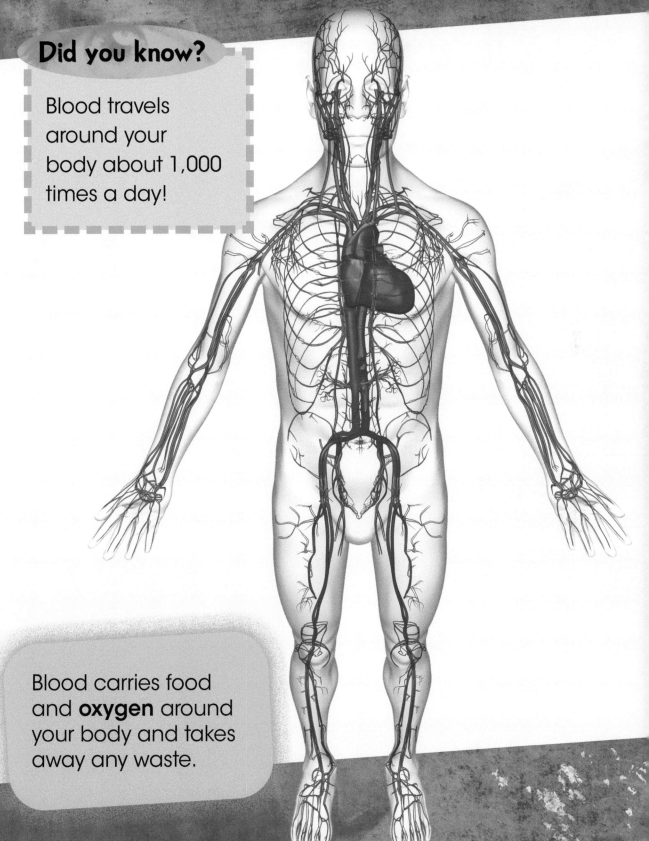

Blood carries food and **oxygen** around your body and takes away any waste.

Muscles

Blood carries food and **oxygen** to your **muscles**. Muscles need food and oxygen to work. Many muscles help you move. Muscles usually work in pairs to help you move. One muscle tightens, while the other muscle relaxes.

pair of arm muscles

Some muscles work without you realizing it. The muscles that push food into your **stomach** work without you having to think about it.

Stomach and Intestines

Let's follow the food into the **stomach**. The stomach pushes the food bit by bit into the small **intestine**. Here it is broken up into even smaller pieces. Healthy parts of the food are carried away in the blood. The food your body does not want goes into the large intestine.

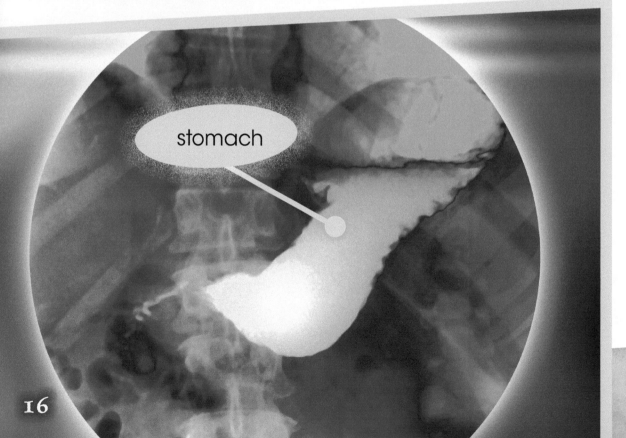

stomach

Did you know?

Any food in the large intestine is made into **feces**, or poop.

stomach

small intestine

large intestine

Kidneys

We are off to the **kidneys** next. The kidneys remove liquid waste, and any water you don't need, from your blood. The waste and water is turned into urine, or pee. You get rid of this when you go to the bathroom.

kidneys

kidney

Urine travels from the kidney to the bladder and then out the body.

Did you know?

A person makes about 12,000 gallons of urine in a lifetime. That is enough to fill 550 bathtubs!

Bones

Without a skeleton, you'd collapse into a pile on the floor! There are 206 bones that make up your skeleton. It supports and protects the **organs** of your body.

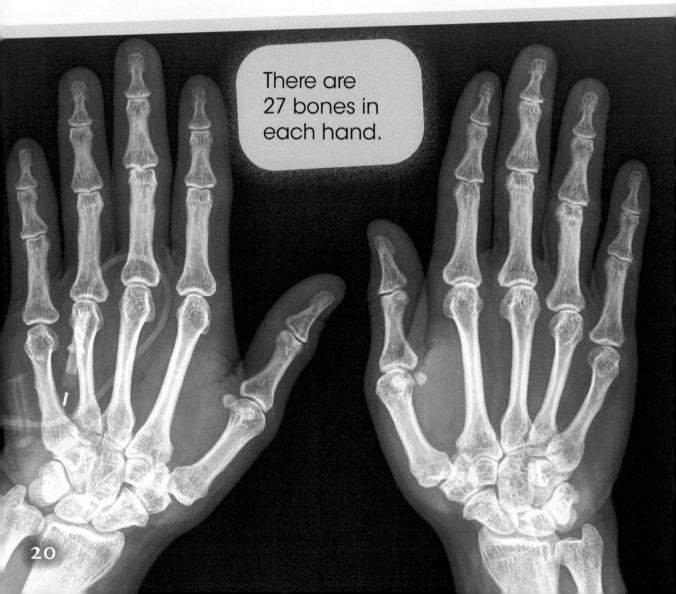

There are 27 bones in each hand.

Did you know?

Babies have about 300 bones, but as they grow up, some bones join together.

Brain

We have reached the control center of the body: the brain! The brain is soft and is protected by a big bone called the skull.

skull

brain

Different parts of the brain control different things.

Did you know?

The brain is used for thinking, learning, and remembering. It also controls what your body does, from talking to walking.

Eyes

Your eyes are for seeing, but you need the brain to help you understand what your eyes see. The **optic nerve** at the back of the eye sends messages about what you see to your brain.

When you look at something, you see it upside down. It is your brain that turns the picture the right way up so that you can recognize it.

what your eyes see

what your brain sees

Ears and Nose

Inside each ear, you can find the smallest bones in the body—the stapes. The stapes **vibrate**, or move, to help you hear.

You use your nose to smell. There is a lot of **mucus** in your nose. You swallow a lot of it. Yuck!

Make sure your rocket doesn't get stuck in the mucus!

Did you know?

When you sneeze, air comes out at 100 miles (160 kilometers) an hour—faster than a car on the highway!

Our Amazing Bodies

We've come to the end of our journey. One **organ** we have not talked about is the one on the outside of our body—skin! Skin is actually your largest organ.

skin

All your bones, **muscles**, and organs work together to help you eat, move, think, and everything else!

Glossary

blood vessel tube that carries blood around the body

cell every part of the body is made up of different types of cells

feces poop

intestines long tubes that take food from your stomach out of your body

kidneys organs in your body that remove waste from your blood and make urine

mucus slimy substance found in the nose

muscle part of the body that helps produce movement

optic nerve part of your body that sends messages about what you see to your brain

organ part of the body that does a special job, such as the heart

oxygen gas that is needed by all living things

platelet tiny blood cell that makes your blood thicker to stop bleeding caused by cuts

saliva watery liquid made in your mouth

stomach organ inside the body where food goes when it is swallowed, and where it is broken into pieces

vibrate shake very quickly

Find Out More

Books

Chandler, Fiona. *First Encyclopedia of the Human Body*. Tulsa, Okla.: EDC, 2010.

Macnair, Patricia Ann. *Building Blocks: Cells, Organs, and Body Systems*. Boston: Kingfisher, 2005.

Stamps, Caroline. *Human Body*. New York: Dorling Kindersley, 2013.

Index